Introduction to 22 Dances

by Harold Bob Jones

The contents of this work, including, but not limited to, the accuracy of events, people, and places depicted; opinions expressed; permission to use previously published materials included; and any advice given or actions advocated are solely the responsibility of the author, who assumes all liability for said work and indemnifies the publisher against any claims stemming from publication of the work.

This book, *Introduction to 22 Dances*, was originally titled *Dance Instructors' and Learners' Introduction to 22 Kinds of Dances (Ballroom, Latin, Country & Western, Ethnic and Line Dances)*. Other changes include an added Table of Contents and Index, plus a few minor improvements in the text.

All Rights Reserved
Copyright © 2019 by Harold Bob Jones

No part of this book may be reproduced or transmitted, downloaded, distributed, reverse engineered, or stored in or introduced into any information storage and retrieval system, in any form or by any means, including photocopying and recording, whether electronic or mechanical, now known or hereinafter invented without permission in writing from the publisher.

Dorrance Publishing Co
585 Alpha Drive
Suite 103
Pittsburgh, PA 15238
Visit our website at *www.dorrancebookstore.com*

ISBN: 978-1-4809-9340-2
eISBN: 978-1-4809-9303-7

FOREWORD

Who is this book for?

If you just want to be able to hold your own in a conversation about dance and/or want to impress yourself and others with how much you know about the kinds of dances, then this book is for you! Better yet, if you actually want to learn how to DO any of these dances quickly and easily, this book is for you! Best yet, if you want to quickly and easily TEACH your significant other or anyone else how to do any of these dances, this book is also for you!

What is this and what isn't it?

It is an introduction to twenty-two kinds of dances. It is not a long, drawn-out manual with lots of photographs, drawings, and other illustrations, videos, etc. showing in great detail how to do lots of steps, positions, etc. of many different dances.

This is designed to give an overview/explanation of these dances, showing in words simply and clearly how these dances are similar to each other and how they differ from each other. It makes it easier for dance instructors and dance learners to understand these dances and how to teach and learn them.

It also clears up a lot of misconceptions about these dances and their history and evolution. Furthermore, it makes dancing and dance instruction easier, more fluid, and less tiring by replacing awkward, clumsy stumble-steps (alias "shuffle"-steps) with triple-steps that move not only leftward and rightward, but also forward and backward – this is done in all dances except the Conga. Additionally, this booklet makes dancing easier and less tiring to learn and do by getting rid of the equal-length quick and slow steps so often taught by many dance studios in the past and even now, replacing those with short-distance quick steps and long-distance slow steps which makes more sense, since there is obviously twice as much time to do slow steps as quick steps!

This also offers a simpler, more logical, more efficient, and more effective sequencing alternative for teaching and learning dances in the order of simple to progressively more difficult than the traditional, virtually random practice of teaching dances all out of order with little if any thought as to their similarity to or difference from each other.

This can be useful to anyone to learn about these twenty-two kinds of dances and how to do them and teach them.

Harold Bob Jones

Table of Contents

Chapter One:
HOW TO DO THE BASIC STEPS OF 22 KINDS OF DANCES

    Part 1: Positioning and Maneuvering   1

    Part 2: How to do "Triple Steps"   2

    Part 3: The Kinds of FOOTWORK in these 22 Dances   4

        Section 1: Dances with only Triple-Steps in their Basic (Traveling) Steps   5

        Section 2: Dances with Triple-Steps plus other steps in their Basic Steps   6

        Section 3: Dances without Triple-Steps in their Basic Steps

    Part 4: The Kinds of TIMING in these 22 Dances   7

    Part 5: Traveling and Non-Traveling Dances   23

    Part 6: Balanced and Unbalanced Dances   24

    Part 7: Review of Differences among Dances   30

    Part 8: The Kinds of BODY-ACTION/STYLING in these 22 Dances   31

Chapter Two:
VARIATIONS (STEPS, POSITIONS, ETC.) OTHER THAN THE BASIC STEPS   35

Index   39

CHAPTER ONE:

HOW TO DO THE BASIC STEPS OF TWENTY-TWO KINDS OF DANCES

First, the dance instructor needs to position the learners properly. A learner needs to stand with his or her feet shoulder-width apart. If his or her feet are too close together, the learner will have balance problems. If the learner's feet are too far apart, he or she will look gawky and clumsy.

Secondly, each learner should stand initially (and dance usually) with his or her left foot slightly farther forward than his or her right foot. This helps the dancer to distinguish between his or her left foot and right foot – the one farther forward is the left foot and the one farther back is the right foot. This greatly reduces the number of foot errors (moving the wrong foot).

Thirdly, the dance instructor needs to position the woman learner slightly to the right of the man learner. If they are toe-to-toe, whoever steps forward will step on his or her partner's foot. The woman should almost always dance with her right foot between her partner's feet. Likewise, the man should almost always dance with his right foot between his partner's feet.

This slight offsetting of the partners to each other's right not only helps keep each other from stepping on each other's feet, but also helps the man to see past the woman so that he can lead her through the other couples on the dance floor and avoid columns, tables, chairs, etc., while allowing the woman to see behind the man (since she is the couple's rear-view mirror) so that she can see any approaching couple and maneuver her partner toward the center of the dance floor, thus allowing more space for the faster couple to dance around to the right of the slower couple (closer to the outside of the dance floor). By the way, in most dances, the dancers dance around the floor in a circle or oval, counter-clockwise (anti-clockwise), with the slower dancers dancing closer to the center and the faster dancers dancing farther from the center of the dance floor. The center of the dance floor is the best and safest place to do showy, but risky lifts, dips, and throws.

Dance instructors especially need to learn how to teach (and dance learners need to learn how to do) the Triple-Step. The Triple-Step is not a kind of dance; it is a kind of footwork used in many kinds of dances. Learning how to do the Triple-Step well will greatly help a person to be able to become a good dancer.

The Triple-Step (and dancing, in general) differs from walking in that, while walking, your left foot and right foot take turns passing each other equally. For example, when you walk, your left foot steps forward with your weight moving on it as it advances, then your right foot passes your left foot with your weight shifting onto it as it advances; then the left foot takes the lead again, then the right foot, and so on. The same is true when walking backwards with each foot passing the other equally, taking turns going farther back than the other foot.

However, in the Triple-Step (and in most dancing), the feet do not pass each other equally. In the Left Forward Triple-Step, your left foot steps substantially forward, and then the right foot steps only slightly forward, but does not pass the left foot; the right foot does not even move as far forward as the left foot has already moved – the right foot in fact moves forward a shorter distance than the left foot has already moved; after both the left foot and the right foot have moved forward, the left foot is still farther ahead than the right foot! Then the left foot steps forward again, this time only slightly (increasing its lead over the right foot), completing a Left Forward Triple-Step (counted: one, two, three; or we can say: left, right, left). By the way, in American ballroom dancing, whoever (man or woman) moves forward initially, does so by stepping forward with the left foot; and whoever (man or woman) moves backward initially, does so with the right foot. Customarily, the man starts dancing by going forward, while the woman usually starts dancing going backward, but they change directions from time to time during the dance.

In a Right Forward Triple-Step (after a Left Forward Triple-Step), the right foot moves forward passing the left foot substantially, then the left foot moves slightly forward, but does not catch up to or pass the right foot (which remains ahead of the left foot), and then the right foot moves slightly farther forward, increasing its lead over the left foot. This completes a Right Forward Triple-Step (counted: four, five, six or spoken as: right, left, right).

In a Right Backward Triple-Step (before a Left Backward Triple-Step), the right foot moves backward, passing substantially farther backward than the left foot, then the left foot moves slightly backward, but not as far backward as (and certainly not passing) the right foot (which remains farther backward than the left foot), and then the right foot moves slightly farther backward, increasing its lead behind the left foot. This completes a Right Backward Triple-Step, which is normally followed by a Left Backward Triple-Step which is similar except that the left foot stays farther back than the right foot throughout the Left Backward Triple-Step.

Sixteen of the twenty-two dances learned in this course have triple-steps in their basic footwork, exclusively or in combination with other kinds of steps (rock-steps, kicks, etc.).

Six of these sixteen dances have only triple-steps in their basic footwork.

Ten of the sixteen dances use both triple-steps and other kinds of steps in their basic footwork.

Six of the twenty-two dances in this course have no triple-steps in their basic footwork, having only other kinds of steps, such as single-steps, double-steps, quadruple-steps, quintuple-steps, rock-steps, kicks, pivots, etc.

The kinds of **FOOTWORK** in the twenty-two dances in this course are shown below:

DANCES WITH ONLY TRIPLE-STEPS IN THEIR BASIC (TRAVELING) STEPS
1. Polka
2. Two-Step – also called Universal Two-Step to distinguish this from the similar Texas Two-Step

3. Rumba
4. Waltz
5. Samba (Bossa Nova/Cumbia)
6. Ramwong (Laotian, Thai, and Cambodian paired, but detached-couple line dance also called Lamvong)

DANCES WITH TRIPLE-STEPS PLUS OTHER STEPS IN THEIR BASIC STEPS

1. Texas Two-Step = triple-step + walk
2. Mambo (Salsa) = hold (pause) or heel-strike + triple-step (usually as rock, recover, return)
3. Cha-Cha = rock step + triple-step + (opposite direction) rock-step + triple-step
4. Tush-Push = country & western line dance, based on Cha-Cha, with a forward left rock-step + backward left triple step + backward right rock-step + backward-right-half-turning forward right triple-step (a back crossover) + backward left rock-step + forward-right half-turning forward left triple-step (a back crossover) + backward right rock-step + forward-left-quarter-turning forward right triple step + right-half-turning left pivot-step + right-half-turning right pivot-step (then repeat all)
5. Triple-Step Swing = side triple-step + (opposite direction) side triple-step + rock-step (when doing East-Coast Swing, but with coaster-step when doing West-Coast Swing)
6. Conga = shuffling (passing) triple-step (actually, a triple shuffle-step) + diagonally-backward kick
7. Schottische = side triple-step + kick + (opposite direction)

side triple-step + kick + skip-step (4 times)
8. Slide = side triple-step + kick + (opposite direction) side triple-step + kick + back triple-step + lean back + left quarter-turn
9. Cotton-Eyed Joe = skipping triple-step (polka-style, 8 times) + cross-kick + back triple-step (4 times)
10. Sarawan = triple-step + various other steps (of a wide variety) with a caller/cuer similar to square dancing (This is a paired, but detached-couple line dance from Laos, Thailand, and Cambodia.)

Dances Without Triple-Steps In Their Basic Steps

1. Double-Step Swing = side double-step + (opposite direction) side double-step + rock-step or coaster-step (usually toe-heel, toe-heel, rock-step in East-Coast Swing, but with coaster-step in West-Coast Swing)
2. Single-Step Swing = side single-step + (opposite direction) side single-step + rock-step in East-Coast Swing, but with coaster-step in West-Coast Swing
3. Merengue (Soca/Soka/Bachata) = a quadruple step with four consecutive steps in any direction with the fourth step as a toe-tap (followed by another quadruple step in a different direction, beginning with the previously-tapped toe). Merengue originally had eight steps in any direction, but that form is rare now.
4. Foxtrot (Fox-Trot) = a quadruple step with two walks and two side steps (i.e. walk, walk, side, side)
5. Tango = a quintuple step with long (slinking) walk, long (slinking) walk, short walk, side step, & side draw (ending on

the drawn toe which will then begin the next quintuple step)
6. Asir Sabre-Rifle-Dagger Dance = six steps (left forward step, right forward tap & return, left back tap & return, right forward step with hunkered-down ending, left kick & return, right kick & return)

Dances are distinguished from each other not only by type of basic footwork (single-step, double-step, triple-step, rock-step, kick, etc.), but also by kind of timing (slow steps or quick steps). A quick step, hereinafter abbreviated as Q, is a footstep (movement of the foot) one time during one drum beat. A slow step, hereinafter abbreviated as S, is a footstep (movement of the foot) one time during two drum beats. Dances can sometimes have the same type of footwork but have different timing (and, in a few instances, even have the same type of footwork and the same timing but have different body sway or different intonation/inflection/up-and-down movement/styling.

THE KINDS OF **TIMING** FOR THE TWENTY-TWO DANCES IN THIS COURSE ARE SHOWN BELOW:

Dance	Timing often THOUGHT of as	But often FEELS like	Often COUNTED as	Body Action
1. Polka	QQQ;QQQ	QQS;QQS	One,Two,THRee;Four,Five,SIx	Skipping
2. Universal Two-Step	QQS;QQS	QQS;QQS	One,Two,THREE;Four,Five,SIX	Gliding (no lower-body swaying/waddling)

Introduction to 22 Dances | 7

NOTE: The Polka is a dance claimed to have been originated by the Poles, Czechs, and Germans and may have originated in the mountains along their joint borders. It differs from the Universal Two-Step in that the Polka usually has faster music and skipping action rather than the gliding movement of the Universal Two-Step which is possibly a descendant of the Rumba. Universal Two-Step music is the most commonly written, performed, and recorded slow music (love songs, ballads, etc.) today and for the past thirty-five years or so.

Dance	Timing often THOUGHT of as	But often FEELS like	Often COUNTED as	Body Action
3. Rumba	QQS;QQS	QQS;QQS	One,Two,THREE;Four,Five,SIX	Swaying (Waddling)

NOTE: The main difference between the Universal Two-Step and the Rumba is that in the Universal Two-Step, the dancers' body weight moves onto their feet while they are advancing or retreating (as in walking and in most other dances); however, in the Rumba, the dancers' body weight belatedly transfers from the stationary foot to the advancing or retreating foot, thus producing the hip-sway or waddling usually called Cuban Motion or Latin Rhythm.

Dance	Timing often THOUGHT of as	But often FEELS like	Often COUNTED as	Body Action
4. Waltz	QQQ;QQQ	SQQ;SQQ	One,TWO,THREE;Four,FIVE,SIX	Gliding (Down, UP, UP)
5. Samba	SQS;SQS	SQQ;SQQ	ONE,Two,Three;FOUR,Five,Six	Leaping (UP,Down,Down)

NOTE: The main difference between Waltz (a dance of German/Austrian origin) and Samba (a dance of mixed Brazilian Portuguese, African, and possibly Amerindian origin) is in their intonation/inflection (up-and-down movement). The Waltz has Down, UP, UP (or we can say: Low, HIGH, HIGH) inflection or intonation; whereas the Samba has the opposite intonation or inflection (UP, Down, Down or HIGH, Low, Low). Bossa Nova (Portuguese for "New Beat") was a Samba variant that began in the early 1960s that possibly descended into the Disco dancing of the late 1960s, 1970s, and early 1980s. Spanish speakers call Samba "Cumbia", but it is essentially the same dance with only slightly different variations.

Dance	Timing often THOUGHT of as	But often FEELS like	Often COUNTED as	Body Action
6. Ramwong	QQS;QQS	QQS;QQS	One,Two,THREE;Four,Five,SIX	Swaying (Waddling)

NOTE: The Ramwong (Lamvong) and the Rumba have not only the same timing and counting, but also the same footwork and styling. The Rumba has been thought of as having originated in Cuba, but it is possibly a descendant of the much older Ramwong, which came from south India to Sri Lanka, Cambodia, Laos, and Siam (Thailand), then via Spanish galleons to Manila, Philippines, Mexico, and Cuba. The Universal Two-Step is possibly a simplified descendant of the Rumba, with the flashy, but somewhat difficult hip-swaying, waddling (belated-weight-transfer) Cuban Motion/Latin Rhythm replaced by simple flat-footed, smooth gliding. The Texas Two-Step may be a descendant of the Universal Two-Step, with the Universal Two-Step's second triple-step replaced by a simple walk – see #7 below.

Dance	Timing often THOUGHT of as	But often FEELS like	Often COUNTED as	Body Action
7. Texas Two-Step	QQS;S	QQS;S	One,Two,THRee;FOur	Gliding

NOTE: The Universal Two-Step has two triple steps and no walks, whereas the Texas Two-Step has only one triple-step, followed by one walk. Remember that the timing of the Universal Two-Step is QQS;QQS, whereas the timing of the Texas Two-Step is QQS;S – the walk is a slow step.

Dance	Timing often THOUGHT of as	But often FEELS like	Often COUNTED as	Body Action
8. Mambo (Salsa)	HQQQ;HQQQ	HQQQ;HQQQ	ONE,Two, Three,Four; FIVE, Six, Seven, Eight	Very fast waddling

NOTE: The Mambo was possibly derived from the Rumba, but the Mambo differs somewhat from the Rumba in that the Mambo has a quick Hold (Pause) or Heel-Strike before each of its triple-steps. Also, Mambo music is usually faster than Rumba music and Mambo footwork is more staccato (faster and jerkier). Mambo triple-steps can be rock, recover, return - forward, backward, leftward, or rightward. Like the Rumba, Mambo has waddling body action (belated weight-transfer/Cuban Motion/Latin Rythym).

Dance	Timing often THOUGHT of as	But often FEELS like	Often COUNTED as	Body Action
9. Cha-Cha	QQ,QQQ;Q Q,QQQ	QS,QQS;QS, QQS	One,TWO,Cha-Cha-Cha; Three,FOUR, Cha-Cha-Cha	Waddling

NOTE: The Cha-Cha was possibly derived from the Mambo, which may have descended from the Rumba, a possible descendant of the Ramwong, as mentioned above, and has similar styling, including the waddling (Cuban Motion/Latin Rhythm). However, the Cha-Cha has slightly more complex footwork than the Rumba and the Ramwong, which have only triple-steps, and the Mambo, which has a quick hold (pause) or heel-strike before each triple-step. Despite this seemingly greater complexity, the Cha-Cha flows surprisingly more smoothly than its possible predecessors and is danced more often and by more people than any of the other three dances that it possibly descended from.

Dance	Timing often THOUGHT of as	But often FEELS like	Often COUNTED as	Body Action
10. Tush-Push	QQ,QQQ;QQ,QQQ	QS,QQS;QS,QQS	One,TWO,Cha-Cha-Cha; Three,FOUR,Cha-Cha-Cha	Waddling

NOTE: The Tush-Push, as mentioned above, is a line dance (not a partnered dance) and is, therefore, not danced by couples with opposite footwork (man on left foot when lady on right foot or vice-versa). In the Tush-Push, as in most other line dances, all the dancers (all the men and all the women) are on the same foot at the same time (like marching soldiers). They can be dancing on a vertical or horizontal line or several groups of lines, but all dancers on the dance floor should be on the same foot (left or right) at the same time, and all dancers should be doing exactly the same thing. The Tush-Push is usually done to Country & Western songs that have a Cha-Cha beat.

Dance	Timing often THOUGHT of as	But often FEELS like	Often COUNTED as	Body Action
11. Triple-Step Swing	QQQ,QQQ;QQ,	QQS,QQS;QS	ONE,Two,Three;ONE,Two,Three; One,TWO (or ONE,Two,Three; FOUR,Five,Six; Seven,EIGHT)	Bouncing & Rocking (or Coaster-Stepping)

NOTE: The Triple-Step Swing is a possible descendant of the Cha-Cha. Both dances have two triple-steps, but the Cha-Cha has two rock-steps also, whereas the Triple-Step Swing has only one rock-step. This rock-step can be replaced with a "coaster-step", a diagonally-backward skipping step used also in the Bossa Nova variation of the Samba and in 1950s-style Foxtrot; when this coaster-step is used in Triple-Step Swing (or Double-Step Swing or Single-Step Swing), it is called West-Coast Swing. If the rock-step is used instead, that kind of Triple (or Double or Single)-Step Swing is called East-Coast Swing, which is far more common than West-Coast Swing because rock-steps are much easier to do than coaster-steps. The Triple-Step Swing (East Coast variety) has been thought to have originated in Harlem in New York City, but may have been brought there from New Orleans by African-American dock workers having interacted with Cha-Cha dancing Cuban ship-workers at night clubs in New Orleans. It was previously often called Boogie-Woogie or just Boogie.

Dance	Timing often THOUGHT of as	But often FEELS like	Often COUNTED as	Body Action
12. Conga	QQQ,Q;QQQ,Q	QQQ,S;QQQ,S	ONE,Two,THREE,Four;One,TWO,THREE,Four (or ONE,Two,THREE,Kick;One,TWO,THREE,Kick	Shuffling & Kicking

NOTE: Today, the Conga is danced almost always as a line dance (without a partner), but, originally, the Conga was a partnered dance (danced by couples) and can still be danced that way. Nowadays, though, the Conga is usually formed in a long vertical line (column) alternating with man, woman, man, woman, etc. each behind each other with the line snaking (curving) all around the dance floor. The so-called triple-step used in the Conga is not a true triple-step; it is really a triple shuffle-step because the dancer's feet actually pass each other on every step (with the feet dragging on the floor while moving forward) except on the diagonally-backward kick which is done to the back right after a left triple shuffle-step and to the back left after a right triple shuffle-step. The person at the front of the line makes all kinds of Latin hand-and-arm gestures and determines which way the line winds around the room. After a short while, the lead dancer suddenly detaches from the line and rejoins the line at the back of the line, leaving the person who was the second in line now becoming the lead dancer and gesturing actively while leading the line around in new ways. The Conga is often used to liven up parties.

Dance	Timing often THOUGHT of as	But often FEELS like	Often COUNTED as	Body Action
13. Schottische	QQQ,Q;QQ Q,Q;QQQQ	QQQ,Q;QQ Q,Q;QQQQ	One,Two Three, KICK; One,Two, Three,KICK; Skip,Skip,Skip, SKIP	Gliding, Kicking & Skipping

NOTE: The Schottische is a very old dance mostly danced in the USA now, but perhaps dating back a few hundred years or more to Scotland and the mountains of northern England with possible Teutonic/Nordic roots in Germany and environs. It is mostly danced nowadays by country & western dancers, either as a line (non-partnered) dance or as a partnered dance. When danced with a partner (in couples), it is often called the Sweetheart Schottische. Whether danced with or without a partner, all dancers (men and women) are all on the same foot (right or left) at the same time (like marching soldiers). An easy way to remember how to do the Schottische is to say (while dancing it): right, behind, right, kick; left, behind, left, kick; skip, skip, skip, skip (and then repeat).

Dance	Timing often THOUGHT of as	But often FEELS like	Often COUNTED as	Body Action
14. Slide	QQQ,Q;QQ Q,Q;QQQ,Q Q	QQQ,Q;QQ Q,Q;QQQ,Q Q	OnE,TwO,ThrEE,KICK;OnE,TwO,ThrEE,KICK; OnE,TwO,ThrEE,Lean BAck, Lean FORward & Turn ¼ Left	Gliding, Kicking, Leaning & Turning

NOTE: The Slide is a line dance (not a partnered dance) with all dancers dancing apart and on the same foot (right or left) at the same time. It is a simplified version of the Electric Slide which was so complicated that it quickly ceased to be danced anymore in that way. Both the Electric Slide and the Slide are possibly descendants of the Schottische (See above.), with the Slide being easier and less tiring than the Schottische and the Electric Slide. The Slide was originally danced to country & western music, but is now danced at least as much to pop, rock, and soul music, and when danced with that kind of music, the Slide ending changes from "Lean Back, Lean Forward & Turn ¼ Left" to "Lean Back, Lean Forward, Lean Back Again, Lean Forward & Turn ¼ Left".

Dance	Timing often THOUGHT of as	But often FEELS like	Often COUNTED as	Body Action
15. Cotton-Eyed Joe	QQQ;QQQ;QQ;QQQ	QQQ;QQQ;QQ;QQQ	ONE,Two,Three; FOUR,Five,Six (& One,TWO; One,Two, THREE)	Fast Skipping & Cross Kicking

NOTE: The Cotton-Eyed Joe is a country & western (possibly mixed cowboy and Amerindian/Native American) dance which can be done either as a line dance, non-partnered with all dancers in horizontal lines (man, woman, man, woman, etc. with arms around each other's waists or shoulders) and with all dancers on the same foot (left or right) like marching soldiers. Also, the Cotton-Eyed Joe can be danced by partners (couples), either with both the man and the woman on the same foot (left or right) like marching soldiers or with the man and the woman on opposite foot (man on left foot, woman on right foot and vice-versa) as in almost all other dances.

Dance	Timing often THOUGHT of as	But often FEELS like	Often COUNTED as	Body Action
16. Sarawan	QQS;QQS	QQS;QQS	One,Two,THREE; Four,Five,SIX (& Various Other)	Swaying (Waddling) (& Various Other)

NOTE: The Sarawan (Saravan) is likely a descendant of the Ramwong (Lamvong) and danced mostly in Thailand, Laos, and Cambodia, and, like the Ramwong, is a line dance; however, the dancers are (as in the Ramwong also) paired (dancing as detached couples), with the men dancing on the inside circle or oval and the women dancing on the outside circle or oval. The main difference between the Ramwong and the Sarawan is that, in the Sarawan, there is a "caller" or cuer who shouts out or sings out instructions on what steps or actions the dancers are all to do (do-si-do, dance down low to the floor, stand on one leg, hold your right ear, etc.) as done in square dancing.

Dance	Timing often THOUGHT of as	But often FEELS like	Often COUNTED as	Body Action
17. Double-Step Swing	QQ;QQ;QQ	QQ;QQ;QQ	ONE,Two; THREE, Four;FIVE,Six (or TOE, Heel; TOE,Heel;ROCK,Recover)	Fast Stepping, Turning & Rocking (or Coaster-stepping)

NOTE: The Double-Step Swing (previously often called the Lindy or the Jitterbug) is danced to faster music than the Triple-Step Swing. There just is not time to do triple-steps to each side, so the dancers do only double-steps to each side or, more easily, just toe-heel on each side before doing a rock-step (i.e. the man does a left toe-heel and then a right toe-heel while the woman does a right toe-heel and then a left toe-heel). Double-Step Swing music was very common in the 1940s and 1980s, whereas Triple-Step music was very common in the 1930s, 1970s, 1990s, and early 2000s. (Remember to replace the rock-step of the East-Coast Swing with the coaster-step when doing West-Coast Swing.)

Dance	Timing often THOUGHT of as	But often FEELS like	Often COUNTED as	Body Action
18. Single-Step Swing	SS;QQ or Q,Q;QQ	SS;QQ or Q,Q;QQ	ONe,TWo; THREE,Four	Slow & Fast Stepping, Turning, & Rocking (or Coaster-Stepping)

NOTE: The Single-Step Swing (originally often called just Rock 'N' Roll, then later called Hard Rock 'N' Roll) can be done to fast music (in lieu of the Double-Step Swing) or very fast music, too fast for Double-Step Swing. It can be danced with all steps being in Quick Time, but doing so is very tiring and makes turns, wraps, spins, lifts, and throws very difficult (and more dangerous), so most people nowadays have substituted slow steps for the quick steps to either side (i.e. the man does a left slow side-step and then a right slow side-step before doing his rock-step while the woman does a right slow side-step and then a left slow side-step before her rock-step). Single-Step Swing music was especially common in the 1950s and 1960s before making a comeback in the 1980s. From the 1950s up to the present time, there have always been several Single, Double, and Triple-Step Swing songs produced every year. (Remember to replace the rock-step of the East-Coast Swing with the coaster-step when doing West-Coast Swing.)

Dance	Timing often THOUGHT of as	But often FEELS like	Often COUNTED as	Body Action
19. Merengue	QQQQ	QQQQ	ONE, TWO, THREE, Four	Swaying (Waddling)

NOTE: The Merengue is a dance that began in the Caribbean (and is called Soca or Soka on some of the English and Dutch-speaking islands and, nowadays, is often called Bachata on Spanish-speaking islands and in Central and South America, especially among young people). It does not use triple-steps; it uses quadruple-steps. As in triple-steps, the feet do not usually pass each other during a Merengue quadruple-step, i.e. the left foot stays ahead of the right foot during a left quadruple-step (whether forward or backward) and the right foot stays ahead of the left foot during a forward or backward right quadruple-step. Also, as in triple-steps, during sideways quadruple-steps, the left foot stays farther left than the right foot during a left quadruple-step and the right foot stays farther right than the left foot during a right quadruple-step. (The fourth footstep usually ends on toe to indicate that that foot will now move again, but in a different direction, usually opposite direction from the previous direction.) Merengue was originally done with eight steps in each direction, but that form is rare nowadays, replaced mostly with quadruple-steps and even with rocking double-steps as in the Soca/Soka variation.

Dance	Timing often THOUGHT of as	But often FEELS like	Often COUNTED as	Body Action
20. Foxtrot	SSQQ	SSQQ	OnE,TwO,THREE,FOur	Gliding

NOTE: Like the Merengue, the Foxtrot does not have triple-steps; it has quadruple-steps, but the Foxtrot's quadruple-steps differ from the Merengue's quadruple-steps. (See above and below.) The Foxtrot was named after its creator, Harry Fox, early in the 20th Century, and is not related to an earlier dance (now out of fashion) called the Turkey-Trot. The Foxtrot is actually a simplified version of the Tango which was the global dance sensation at that time. Fox reduced the Tango's quintuple-step (with five foot steps) to just a quadruple-step (with four foot steps), eliminated the slinkiness from the tango's two long slow walks, converted the Tango's short forward quick step into a sideways quick step (to the man's left and woman's right), shifted the Tango's quick sideways step to the opposite side, and eliminated the Tango's slow side draw (step). Because the Foxtrot is so similar to the Tango, but much easier, most dance students have much more success in learning the Tango if they have just finished learning the Foxtrot before starting to learn the Tango. Note, also, that when danced very quickly, often blended with Charleston steps, Foxtrot is usually called "Quick Step". When danced to passionate "Torch Songs", Foxtrot long slow steps are done with low, slinky Tango styling and Foxtrot short quick side steps are done with Rumba styling (waddling body action/belated weight transfer/Cuban Motion/Latin Rhythm); when danced this way, Foxtrot is often called "Foxy".

Dance	Timing often THOUGHT of as	But often FEELS like	Often COUNTED as	Body Action
21. Tango	SSQQS	SSQQS	ONe, TWo, Three, Four, FIve	Slinky Gliding

NOTE: The Tango originated in Argentina and does not have triple-steps; it has a quintuple-step (five foot steps) during eight drum beats, the only dance to do so. As mentioned in the paragraph above, the Foxtrot was derived from the Tango; both are "L"-shaped dances; however, the Foxtrot goes forward and then leftward initially for the man while the woman initially goes backward and then rightward, whereas the Tango moves forward and then rightward initially for the man with the woman initially moving backward and then leftward; that is, the Tango and Foxtrot have the same-direction beginning, but opposite-direction ending.

Dance	Timing often THOUGHT of as	But often FEELS like	Often COUNTED as	Body Action
22. Asir Sabre-Rifle-Dagger Dance	QQQQQQ	QQQQQQ	OnE, TwO, ThrEE, FoUR, FiVE, SIx	Stepping, Dragging, Tapping, & Kicking

NOTE: The Asir Sabre-Rifle-Dagger Dance is a dance called Al-Khutwa in Arabic and was originally done in the mountain villages of Yemen and the southwestern Saudi Arabian Province of Asir, but is now done all over Saudi Arabia and Yemen, especially on important occasions. This dance has no triple-steps. It has six steps, even-speeded. This dance is a line dance (not a partnered dance), danced usually in horizontal lines by only males or only females, never mixed sexes. The dancers can be attached with interlocking arms around each other's waists or shoulders, or they can be detached, dancing as separated individuals, though usually still in a horizontal line. When dancing apart, individual dancers often dance holding, in the right hand, a long sabre sword (held vertically, pointed upward), a long old-fashioned rifle (held vertically, pointed upward), or a large (wide/thick) but usually short curved dagger (held vertically, but pointed downward). In Arabic, the dagger is called a "jambiyya", and many foreigners in Saudi Arabia and neighboring Yemen refer to this dance as the Jambiyya Dance.

TRAVELING AND NON-TRAVELING DANCES

TRAVELING DANCES: The following twelve dances usually travel around and around the dance floor except when the way is blocked by too many other dancers, at which time the dancers have no choice but to dance in place (with forward & backward steps, leftward & rightward side steps, right & left turns in place, box steps, etc.) until the way ahead becomes unblocked and they can then resume traveling around and around the dance floor. These dances are:

1. Polka
2. Universal Two-Step
3. Texas Two-Step
4. Waltz
5. Samba (Bossa Nova/Cumbia)
6. Foxtrot
7. Tango
8. Cotton-Eyed Joe
9. Schottische
10. Ramwong
11. Sarawan
12. Conga

NON-TRAVELING DANCES: The following ten dances do NOT usually travel around and around the dance floor, although they can sometimes travel a little to move onto the dance floor, to move closer to or farther away from the music source, or to move to a less-crowded part of the dance floor. Usually these dances stay in basically the same part of the dance floor, though they do move a bit forward and backward, leftward and rightward, turn right and left, and use box-steps, rock-steps, kick-steps, etc. These dances are:

1. Rumba
2. Mambo (Salsa)
3. Cha-Cha
4. Triple-Step Swing
5. Double-Step Swing
6. Single-Step Swing
7. Merengue (Soca/Soka/Bachata)
8. Slide
9. Tush-Push
10. Asir Sabre-Rifle-Dagger Dance (Al-Khutwa)

BALANCED DANCES AND UNBALANCED DANCES

Balanced (symmetric or symmetrical) Dances are dances that have the same thing happening on both the left and right sides of the footwork. All six of the dances that have only triple-steps in their basic (traveling) steps are balanced, with #s 1-5 below having footwork for the man initially as Left Forward Triple-step followed by Right Forward Triple-step and for the woman initially as Right Back Triple-step followed by Left Back Triple-step. (Instead, the man can do a Left Side [sideways] Triple-step followed by a Right Side Triple-step while the woman does a Right Side Triple-step followed by a Left Side Triple-step, and so on.) However it is done, there is a triple-step on each side, Left and Right or Right and Left, whether forward, backward, or sideways, or even if the triple-steps are shaped into the form of a box (as box-steps).

These six Balanced Dances are:

1. Polka
2. Universal Two-Step
3. Rumba
4. Waltz
5. Samba (Bossa Nova/Cumbia)
6. Ramwong differs from #s1-5 above in that Ramwong is basically a Balanced LINE Dance (from Southeast Asia) with the man and the woman paired side-by-side, but detached, both dancing only forward with the man doing a left triple-step followed by right triple-step, etc. while the woman does a right triple-step followed by a left triple-step, etc.

Other Balanced Dances include:

7. Mambo (Salsa) with the man's footwork as Right Hold (Pause) or Heel-strike, Left Rock Forward (or Leftward), Right Recover (Pick up the Right Foot and set it back down in the same place), and Left Backward Return (to its original location, but now ending on the Left Toe) followed by Left Hold (Pause) or Heel-strike, Right Rock Back (or Rightward), Left

Recover, and Right Forward Return (on toe). The woman's footwork is Left Hold (Pause) or Heel-strike, Right Rock Back (or Rightward), Left Recover, and Right Forward Return (on toe) followed by Right Hold (Pause) or Heel-strike, Left Rock Forward (or Leftward), Right Recover, and Left Backward return (on toe). Note that the first half of the man's Mambo footwork combination is exactly the same as the second half of the woman's footwork and her first half is the same as his second half.

NOTE: This his/her first-half/second-half mirroring occurs also in box-steps, whether of the Universal Two-Step and Rumba type (man's left, left, forward; then right, right, backward and woman's right, right, backward; then left, left forward) or the box-step used in the Waltz, Samba (Bossa/Nova Cumbia), and Mambo (Salsa): man forward, right, right; then backward, left, left and woman backward, left, left; then forward, right, right, right.

NOTE: This his/her first-half/second-half mirroring occurs also in the Cha-Cha. (See #8 below.)

8. Cha-Cha is also a Balanced Dance as the man's footwork is initially Left Rock Forward, Right Recover, Left Back Triple-step followed by Right Rock Back, Left Recover, Right Forward Triple-step while the woman's footwork is initially Right Rock Back, Left Recover, Right Forward

Triple-step followed by Left Rock Forward, Right Recover, Left Back Triple-step. These triple-steps can be either forward and backward or leftward and rightward. Note again that his first half is the same as her second half and her first half is the same as his second half.

9. Merengue (Soca/Soka/Bachata) is another Balanced Dance, but with waddling quadruple steps for the man initially as Left, Left, Left, Tap; Right, Right, Right, Tap (or Forward, Forward, Forward, Tap; Back, Back, Back, Tap) with the woman having the opposite footwork as initially Right, Right, Right, Tap; Left, Left, Left, Tap (or Back, Back, Back, Tap; Forward, Forward, Forward, Tap). The Soca/Soka variation is, for the man, Waddle Forward, Waddle Backward while the woman does Waddle Backward, Waddle Forward. Bachata is just a more-pronounced hip-sway version of Merengue with some extra variations.

10. Conga is a Balanced Dance usually danced as a vertical line (column) with man behind woman behind man, etc. and with all dancers on the same foot (left or right) at the same time doing a left forward triple-shuffle-step followed by a right diagonally backward kick and then a right forward triple-shuffle-step followed by a left diagonally backward kick.

11. Sarawan is basically a Balanced Dance, the same as the Ramwong (#6) above, but with occasional unbalanced steps, as called by the caller/cuer (as in square dancing).

Unbalanced (asymmetric or asymmetrical) Dances are dances that do NOT have the same thing happening on both the left and right (or forward and backward) sides of the footwork. In most Balanced Dances, the man and the woman both step off initially on the left foot when going forward or leftward and step off initially on the right foot when going backward or rightward. However, in Unbalanced Dances, only the man steps off initially on the left foot whether going forward, backward, leftward or rightward; whereas only the woman steps off initially on the right foot whether going forward, backward, leftward, or rightward.

Unbalanced Dances include the following:

1. Texas Two-Step which has a triple-step on one side, but only a walk on the other side,
2. Triple-Step Swing which has a triple-step on both left and right sides, but only a back rock-step (or coaster-step), no forward rock-step (or coaster-step),
3. Double-Step Swing which has a double-step on both left and right sides, but only a back rock-step (or coaster-step), no forward rock-step (or coaster-step),
4. Single-Step Swing which has a single-step on both left and right sides, but only a back rock-step (or coaster-step), no forward rock-step (or coaster-step),
5. Foxtrot which has a quadruple-step with the man going forward, forward, left, left or backward, backward, left, left, but he never goes forward, forward, right, right or backward, backward, right, right. The woman goes back-

ward, backward, right, right or forward, forward, right, right, but never backward, backward, left, left or forward, forward, left, left,

6. Tango which has a quintuple-step with the man going forward, forward, forward, right, right or backward, backward, backward, right, right, but he never goes forward, forward, forward, left, left or backward, backward, backward, left, left. The woman goes backward, backward, backward, left, left, or forward, forward, forward, left, left, but never backward, backward, backward, right, right or forward, forward, forward, right, right),

7. Cotton-Eyed Joe which has eight forward triple-steps (but no backward triple-steps) and then cross-kick-back-back-back four times (but no cross-kick-forward-forward-forward four times),

8. Schottische which has right-right-right-kick, left-left-left kick, but then only four forward skip-steps, no backward skip-steps,

9. Slide which has right-right-right-kick, left-left-left-kick, but only back-back-back, lean back, and quarter-turn left; but no forward, forward, forward, lean forward, and quarter-turn right,

10. Tush-Push (See page 3 #4 above for footwork) which starts balanced, but finishes (before repeating) with a quarter-turn left, no quarter-turn right,

11. Asir Sabre-Rifle-Dagger Dance (Al-Khutwa) which seems like a Balanced Dance (See explanations on Page 4 #6), but has only "right forward step with hunkered-down ending", no "left forward step with hunkered-down ending" or "right backward step with hunkered-down ending".

SUMMARY OF BALANCED AND UNBALANCED DANCES

Balanced Dances:	Unbalanced Dances:
1. Polka	1. Texas Two-Step
2. Universal Two-Step	2. Triple-Step Swing
3. Rumba	3. Double-Step Swing
4. Waltz	4. Single-Step Swing
5. Samba (Bossa Nova/Cumbia)	5. Foxtrot
6. Ramwong	6. Tango
7. Mambo (Salsa)	7. Cotton-Eyed Joe
8. Cha-Cha	8. Schottische
9. Merengue (Soca/Soka/Bachata)	9. Slide
10. Conga	10. Tush-Push
11. Sarawan	11. Asir Sabre-Rifle-Dagger Dance (Al-Khutwa)

REVIEW OF DIFFERENCES AMONG DANCES

Remember that dances differ from one another either in footwork (See Pages 3-6 and 13-16.) or in timing (See Pages 6-12.). Dances may also differ from one another in body-action, the main component in styling (which includes hand gestures, carriage/posture, mannerisms, etc.). Dances can have the same footwork, but different timing and different body-action, for example Polka and Universal Two-Step. Or, dances can have the same footwork and same/similar timing, but different body-action, for example Rumba compared to Universal Two-Step or Waltz compared to Samba (Bossa Nova / Cumbia). Dances can also have the same body-action, but different footwork and different timing, such as Universal Two-Step compared to Texas Two-Step. Dances can even have different timing, different footwork, AND different body-action, such as Mambo (Salsa) compared to Tango or Slide compared to Foxtrot!

The kinds of **BODY-ACTION/STYLING** for the twenty-two dances in this course are shown below:

1. Polka – skipping; lots of upper-body sway if Country & Western music, none if Latin music
2. Universal Two-Step – gliding (flat-footed, smooth, no skipping or lurching); some upper-body sway, no lower-body sway (waddling)
3. Texas Two-Step – gliding (flat-footed, smooth, no skipping or lurching); lots of upper-body sway, no lower-body sway (waddling)
4. Rumba – waddling (belated weight-transfer/Cuban Motion/Latin Rhythm); no upper-body sway, lots of lower-body sway; classic Latin styling
5. Waltz – gliding, but with intonation/inflection as Down, Up, Up (Low, High, High; Flat, Toe, Toe); lots of swirling, whirling, & turning, especially in Viennese waltz; lots of box-steps, traveling and turning, in ordinary waltz; lots of traveling triple-steps in country & western waltz
6. Samba (Bossa Nova/ Cumbia) – leaping, with intonation/inflection as Up, Down, Down (High, Low, Low); some upper-body sway, lots of lower-body sway; combined Latin and African styling

7. Mambo (Salsa) – very fast waddling (belated weight-transfer/Cuban Motion/Latin Rhythm), staccato (faster and jerkier than Rumba and Cha-Cha); very little upper-body sway, lots of lower-body sway; classic Latin styling
8. Cha-Cha – waddling (belated weight-transfer/Cuban Motion/Latin Rhythm), faster waddling than Rumba, but slower than Mambo (Salsa); very little upper-body sway, lots of lower-body sway; classic Latin styling
9. Tush-Push - same as Cha-Cha (See #8 above.)
10. Triple-Step Swing – bouncy waddling (on the side steps), turning, and rocking or coaster-stepping; man & woman face each other during triple-steps, but during rock-steps or coaster-steps, man faces left & woman faces right
11. Double-Step Swing – Lindy: fast hopping (side-side, opposite side-side, backward-forward); Jitterbug: fast stepping, turning, and rocking or coaster-stepping (toe-heel, toe-heel, rock-recover or coaster-step); man & woman face each other during double-steps, but during rock-steps or coaster-steps, man faces left & woman faces right
12. Single-Step Swing – slow (or very fast) stepping (on the side-steps) and very fast turning and rocking or coaster-stepping; man & woman face each other during sideways single-steps, but during rock-steps or coaster-steps, man faces left & woman faces right
13. Merengue – even-speeded waddling (belated weight-transfer/Cuban Motion/Latin Rhythm); very little upper-body sway, lots of lower-body sway; classic Latin styling

14. Foxtrot – usually gliding (flat-footed, smooth, no skipping or lurching), but the "Quick-Step" speeded-up version of the Foxtrot has perky, almost bouncy, fast gliding (mixed with Charleston steps) and the "Foxy" version of the Foxtrot danced to steamy "torch songs" has bent-knee, low, slinky Tango styling during the two long forward or backward slow steps and Rumba-style waddling (belated weight-transfer/Cuban Motion/Latin Rhythm) during the two short quick left or right side steps
15. Tango – slinky gliding with bent knees, especially on the long slow steps; very erect posture, close together at the waist and below, but leaning away from each other above the waist with man's left and woman's right arm far out (but not locked elbows)
16. Slide – gliding, kicking, and leaning with whatever styling the individual wishes to add (including various hand-and-arm gestures, swaying, boot-stomping, etc.)
17. Schottische – gliding, kicking, and skipping
18. Cotton-Eyed Joe – fast forward skipping (Polka-style), cross-kicking, and backward stepping
19. Conga – shuffling (forward) and diagonally kicking (backward) with combined Latin and African styling
20. Ramwong – waddling (belated weight-transfer/Cuban Motion/Latin Rhythm); very little upper-body sway, lots of lower-body sway; Latin-type styling
21. Sarawan – same as Ramwong (See #20 above.), except for whatever quirky variations are called for by the "caller/cuer" as in square dancing

22. Asir Sabre-Rifle-Dagger Dance (Al-Khutwa) – stepping, dragging, tapping, and kicking

CHAPTER TWO:
VARIATIONS (STEPS, POSITIONS, ETC.) OTHER THAN THE BASIC STEPS IN CHAPTER ONE

(Unless otherwise marked below, these steps, positions, etc. are used in most dances other than line dances.)

To save space, the following abbreviations are used:
- M = Man
- W = Woman
- F = Forward
- B = Backward
- L = Left
- R = Right
- C = Continuous

CP = Closed Position, **SCP** = Semi-Closed Position,
SOP = Semi-Open Position, **OP** = Open Position,
OLP = Offset Left Position, **ORP** = Offset Right Position,
Butterfly = Two-Handed, Facing OP with upward hand hold,
LBW = Left Back Wrap, **RHW** = Right Hip Wrap,
RWW = Right Waist Wrap, **LWW** = Left Waist Wrap,
LSW = Left Shoulder Wrap (Left Varsuvian Position),
RSW = Right Shoulder Wrap (Right Varsuvian Position),
DNW = Double-Neck Wrap, **MW** = Man's Wrap

1. M&W CP, M&W SCP, M&W SOP, M&W OP, M&W OLP, & M&W ORP
2. W LBW, W RHW, W RWW, W LWW, W LSW, W RSW, M&W DNW, & MW
3. M&W, F&B Traveling Step (in all positions & wraps) (In-line & L&R Turning)
4. M&W, F&B, L&R, ¼, ½, ¾, 1, 1 ½, 2, 2 ½, 3, 4, 5, & C Turn (in all positions & wraps, especially CP)
5. M&W, F&B, L&R, ½, 1, 2, 3, 4, 5, & C Underarm Turn (in all positions & wraps except SOP)
6. M&W, F&B, L&R Spin Turn (in OP, 1-handed & 2-handed)
7. M&W, L&R, Side Step (In-place & L&R Turning) (in CP)
8. M&W, F&B, L&R, ½ & Full Box Step (in CP) (in "balanced" dances only, e.g. Universal Two-Step, Waltz, Rumba, & Samba, except Polka) (In-place & L&R Turning)
9. M&W, F&B, L&R Balance Step (In-place, Traveling, & L&R Turning) (in CP & Butterfly) (in Samba/Cumbia & slow Waltz)
10. M&W, F&B, L&R Zig-Zag (in CP, OLP, ORP, Butterfly, LSW & RSW)
11. M&W, F&B, L&R Lock Step (in all positions)
12. M&W, F, L&R Cutaway Step (in SCP, SOP, & OP)
13. M&W, F&B, L&R Twinkle Step (in CP) (in Waltz & Foxtrot Only)

14. M&W, F&B, L&R, Dance Around (in CP to OP to CP) (in Rumba & Waltz)
15. M&W, F&B, L&R, Crossover (Front-Front in OP, Front-Back in ORP & OLP, Back-Back in SCP & OP, & Back-Front in OLP & ORP) (in Rumba, Mambo/Salsa, Cha-Cha, & slow Waltz)

INDEX

Following is an alphabetical listing of the 22 dances in this book and the pages on which each dance is mentioned in each Chapter, Part, and Section of the book:

Al-Khutwa (Asir Sabre-Rifle-Dagger Dance   7, 22, 24, 29, 30, 34
Bachata (Merengue/Soca/Soka)   6, 19, 20, 24, 27, 30, 32
Bossa Nova (Samba/Cumbia)   5, 9, 13, 23, 25, 30, 31, 36
Cha-Cha   5, 11, 12, 13, 24, 26, 30, 32, 37
Conga   5, 13, 14, 23, 27, 30, 33
Cotton-Eyed Joe   6, 16, 23, 29, 30, 33
Cumbia (Samba/Bossa Nova)   5, 9, 13, 23, 25, 30, 31, 36
Double-Step Swing   6, 13, 17, 18, 19, 24, 28, 30, 32
Foxtrot   6, 13, 20, 21, 23, 28, 30, 31, 33, 36
Mambo (Salsa)   5, 10, 11, 24, 25, 26, 30, 31, 32, 37
Merengue (Soca/Soka/Bachata)   6, 19, 20, 24, 27, 30, 32
Polka   4, 6, 7, 8, 23, 25, 30, 31, 33, 36
Ramwong   5, 9, 10, 11, 17, 25, 27, 30, 33
Rumba   5, 8, 9, 10, 11, 21, 24, 25, 26, 30, 31, 32, 33, 36, 37
Salsa (Mambo)   5, 10, 11, 24, 25, 26, 30, 31, 32, 37
Samba (Bossa Nova/Cumbia)   5, 9, 12, 23, 25, 30, 31, 36
Sarawan   6, 17, 23, 30, 33
Schottische   5, 6, 14, 15, 16, 23, 29, 30, 33
Single-Step Swing   6, 13, 18, 19, 24, 28, 30, 32
Slide   6, 15, 16, 24, 27, 30, 32

Soca/Soka (Merengue/Bachata)	6, 19, 20, 24, 27, 30, 32
Tango	6, 7, 20, 21, 23, 29, 30, 31, 33
Texas-Two Step	5, 10, 23, 28, 30, 31
Triple Step-Swing	5, 12, 13, 17, 18, 19, 24, 28, 30, 32
Tush-Push	5, 12, 24, 29, 30, 32
Universal Two-Step	4, 8, 10, 23, 25, 26, 30, 31, 36
Waltz	5, 9, 23, 25, 26, 30, 31, 36, 37